# Remembering
# Austin

## Marsia Hart Reese

TURNER
PUBLISHING COMPANY

The Post Office took ten years to build and was completed in 1880 at the corner of Pecan (Sixth) and Colorado streets. Also called the Federal Building because of its federal courtrooms, it was where the embezzlement trial of William Sydney Porter (O. Henry) was held. That's why it is now called O. Henry Hall. Next door (at right) was the splendid Hancock Opera House, which opened in 1896, and behind was the Masonic Temple.

# Remembering
# Austin

Turner Publishing Company

*Remembering Austin*

www.turnerpublishing.com

Copyright © 2010 Turner Publishing Company

Library of Congress Control Number: 2010902286

ISBN: 978-1-59652-612-9

Printed in the United States of America

ISBN 978-1-68442-240-1

# CONTENTS

ACKNOWLEDGMENTS.................................................VII

PREFACE ............................................................VIII

AN AUSPICIOUS LOCATION
(1838–1899).................................................... 1

ERA OF PROGRESS
(1900–1919)................................................... 41

ELATION AND DEPRESSION
(1920–1940)................................................... 77

WAR, PEACE, AND ACTIVISM
(1941–1969).................................................. 121

NOTES ON THE PHOTOGRAPHS ................................. 132

After the Austin Dam was built, creating Lake McDonald, Austinites and visitors enjoyed many a ride on the lake aboard the *Ben Hur,* a pleasure-cruise steamboat. For 50 cents, one could take a tour that lasted more than three hours, and dances were frequently held on the decks after sundown. The *Ben Hur* was literally grounded during the flood of 1900.

# ACKNOWLEDGMENTS

This volume, *Remembering Austin*, is the result of the cooperation and efforts of many individuals and organizations. It is with great thanks that we acknowledge the valuable contribution of the following for their generous support:

Austin History Center
Library of Congress
Lyndon Baines Johnson Library and Museum
Texas State Library and Archives Commission

We would also like to thank the following individuals for their valuable contributions and assistance in making this work possible:

Marsia Hart Reese, Writer and Editor
John Anderson, Archives and Information Services, Texas State Library

# PREFACE

Austin has thousands of historic photographs that reside in archives, both locally and nationally. This book began with the observation that, while those photographs are of great interest to many, they are not easily accessible. During a time when Austin is looking ahead and evaluating its future course, many people are asking, How do we treat the past? These decisions affect every aspect of the city—architecture, public spaces, commerce, and infrastructure—and these, in turn, affect the way that people live their lives. This book seeks to provide easy access to a valuable, objective look into the history of Austin.

The power of photographs is that they are less subjective than words in their treatment of history. Although the photographer can make subjective decisions regarding subject matter and how to capture and present it, photographs seldom interpret the past to the extent textual histories can. For this reason, photography is uniquely positioned to offer an original, untainted look at the past, allowing the viewer to learn for himself what the world was like a century or more ago.

This project represents countless hours of review and research. The researchers and writer have reviewed thousands of photographs in numerous archives. We greatly appreciate the generous assistance of the individuals and organizations listed in the acknowledgments of this work, without whom this project could not have been completed.

The goal in publishing this work is to provide broader access to this set of extraordinary photographs that seek to inspire, provide perspective, and evoke insight that might assist people who are responsible for determining Austin's future. In addition, the book seeks to preserve the past with adequate respect and reverence.

With the exception of touching up imperfections that have accrued with the passage of time and cropping where necessary, no changes have been made. The focus and clarity of many images is limited by the technology and the ability of the photographer at the time they were taken.

The work is divided into eras. Beginning with some of the earliest known photographs of Austin, the first section records photographs from before the Civil War through the end of the nineteenth century. The second section spans the beginning of the twentieth century through World War I. Section Three moves from World War I to World War II. The last section covers from World War II to the 1970s.

In each of these sections we have made an effort to capture various aspects of life through our selection of photographs. People, commerce, transportation, infrastructure, religious institutions, and educational institutions have been included to provide a broad perspective.

We encourage readers to reflect as they go walking in Austin, strolling through the city, its parks, and its neighborhoods. It is the publisher's hope that in utilizing this work, longtime residents will learn something new and that new residents will gain a perspective on where Austin has been, so that each can contribute to its future.

*—Todd Bottorff, Publisher*

This view shows the 1853 Texas Capitol at the head of Congress Avenue in the early 1870s. By this time, some people were criticizing the statehouse as lacking distinction. Private businesses and government buildings with limestone and brick facades lined "the Avenue," along with saloons such as the Iron Front. This capitol burned in 1881, and plans soon began for building a bigger and better one.

# An Auspicious Location

## (1838–1899)

Austin's volunteer fire department was organized by John Bremond and William Walsh in the summer of 1858 as Hook and Ladder Company Number One. The fire station pictured here, built later, was on Hickory (Eighth Street) next to City Hall. A local newspaper noted in 1881, "The most prominent bankers, merchants, and professional men in Austin are firemen."

This imposing three-story structure with raised basement opened in March 1861 at what was then the northern outskirts of town. Texas's oldest hospital for the mentally ill, it was originally called the State Lunatic Asylum, but later the name was changed to the more humane Austin State Hospital. On opening day there were approximately 12 resident patients.

After the Civil War, freed African-Americans quickly set about organizing schools and churches. The Wesley Chapel Methodist Episcopal Church was founded in March 1865, the first formally organized African-American church in Austin. The permanent sanctuary pictured was later constructed at the southeast corner of San Antonio and Ninth streets.

In its early years, Pecan Street sported a variety of businesses in simple frame buildings of one or two stories.

On January 2, 1872, the first bale of cotton was shipped out of Austin by rail, just a week after the first train arrived. Cotton was an important cash crop, and the railroad's appearance ensured a burgeoning market for products of the fertile soil of Central Texas. This photograph shows a cotton gin on a farm outside Austin.

The previous Travis County Courthouse, completed in 1876, stood quite grandly at the east corner of Congress Avenue and Eleventh (Mesquite) Street. The Capitol would be completed 12 years later across Eleventh Street (to the left) facing Congress. A new courthouse was built in the 1930s several blocks west on Guadalupe Street and is still in use today.

This 1879 view of Pecan (Sixth) Street looks east from Colorado Street. Eight years earlier, the arrival of the railroad had sparked a commercial boom. Victorian-style limestone business buildings proliferated, and a cluster of African-American businesses began east of East Avenue, Austin's first eastern boundary street, which in later years would become Interstate 35, a busy highway.

During Austin's first 45 years, citizens received medical care either at home, in private infirmaries, or in "pest camps" set aside for treating contagious diseases. In 1884, this public hospital was built on the farthest northeast lot of the original city's plan. The first public hospital in Texas, it could treat up to 40 patients, and a private room cost up to $2.50 a day. The city's Brackenridge Hospital occupies the same site today.

Workers prepare to place the formidable-looking *Goddess of Liberty* statue atop the Capitol's dome, where she would remain for almost a century. The newly completed building was dedicated in the spring of 1888, and in the mid-1980s, the statue was brought back down for reinforcement during the statehouse's major renovation.

"Old Main" was the first building on the University of Texas campus. Before it was completed in the summer of 1884, classes were held in the temporary Capitol, which was on the southeast corner of Congress Avenue at Eleventh (Mesquite) Street, across from the permanent Capitol's site, which faces Eleventh.

When it was established in 1876, Temple Beth Israel, Austin's first Jewish congregation, was about 30 families. Services were held at Mr. Sampson's Hall or the Odd Fellows Hall until this handsome stone synagogue was completed in 1884 at the corner of Mesquite (Eleventh) and San Jacinto streets.

Early on, Pecan Street (Sixth Street) became a market center because of its location near the railroad and because it was wide and flat enough for a horse team and wagon to turn around in comfortably. This photograph shows a row of retail establishments on the street circa 1880, before the streetcar tracks were laid and before it was paved with bricks.

This iron bridge with stone supports, called the Corporation Bridge, spanned the Colorado River in 1884, replacing a wooden bridge that had collapsed in 1883. The iron bridge was replaced in 1910 by a concrete one, which still stands as the Congress Avenue Bridge. It is home to thousands of bats, which at sunset swarm out from under the bridge en masse, attracting tourists and local citizens alike.

On the morning of May 16, 1888, the new Capitol's dedication day, crowds had gathered by eight-thirty. Early birds grabbed seats on the ledge of the second story, where they could watch the dedication ceremonies and the mile-long parade headed by the Masonic Grand Lodge of Texas. An entire week of planned festivities and entertainment included fireworks, bands, and displays by military drill teams from across the country.

Photographer S. B. Hill took this photograph looking down Congress Avenue from the Capitol grounds circa 1888. The fence was a temporary structure while the new Capitol was under construction (in the foreground, parallel to Eleventh Street). The imposing building at left is the Travis County Courthouse. The Lundberg Bakery building is in the first block on the right.

The Texas Capitol has been Austin's best-known landmark since its completion in 1888. For many years it towered above all other buildings in town, dominating the landscape.

When the Capitol was completed, photographers took their cameras to its dome to capture the spectacular views. This shot looking south shows Congress Avenue, right, and Brazos Street, left. The Travis County Courthouse is at the corner of Congress and Eleventh. The Methodist Church and St. Mary's Cathedral face each other at the corner of Brazos and Tenth. Stone turrets identify the Travis County Jail.

This view from the Capitol dome looks southwest of Congress Avenue. The large three-story building at center is the temporary Capitol, used while the 1888 Capitol was under construction. The steepled building at right is the Tenth Street Baptist Church.

This view from the Capitol dome looking east shows the residential area that would become home to many of Austin's African-American and Mexican-American families in the twentieth century.

The view from the Capitol dome looking west shows many of the grand Victorian homes that would be torn down in the twentieth century to make room for businesses including parking garages.

This view of Congress Avenue in the 1890s was taken from the roof of the Travis County Courthouse, which was across Eleventh (Mesquite) Street from the Capitol. The Colorado River is visible in the distance. The Lundberg Bakery building, lower right corner, is identifiable by its triple arches and the brass eagle atop its pediment.

Austin has long been home to music festivals, thanks in no small part to its settlers of German descent. This temporary archway on Congress Avenue was erected in 1889 to welcome German singers from across Texas to a saengerfest, or songfest. The Saengerrunde, a German folk-singing society, had been founded a decade earlier. The club practiced at Scholz's beer garden, still home to this traditional style of singing.

In the 1890s, young ladies could enjoy feeding the ducks near Gem Lake's landscaped central island on Sunday afternoon outings in Hyde Park, the residential community developed by Monroe Martin Shipe. Shipe had come to Austin from Kansas in 1889 to install the city's new streetcar railway system, and he stayed to develop his "elegant suburb," which was then more than a mile outside the city limits.

Austin National Bank opened its doors on June 16, 1890, in a leased space on the ground floor of the Hancock Building. Several law offices occupied spaces on upper floors. This building was in the 100 block of Pecan (now West Sixth) Street, which means it was just around the corner from Congress Avenue.

25

The First National Bank of Austin stood proudly at the northwest corner of Congress Avenue and Sixth (Pecan) Street.

This photograph captured men hard at work laying track for the new electric streetcars at the corner of Sixth Street and Congress Avenue.

The Hyde Park Transit Pavilion, an open-air structure built in 1892, was owned by the street railway company whose streetcars regularly ran to it from town and back. The pavilion offered all kinds of entertainment: dances, puppet shows, plays, and musical performances such as Gilbert and Sullivan's *HMS Pinafore* by the Austin Musical Union.

Construction is in progress on the first Austin Dam, completed in 1893. Its proponents envisioned that dam-generated electric power would transform Austin into a manufacturing center, but poor research before the dam's construction caused problems later. Electricity did not flow until 1895, a power shortfall in 1899 was so great that water and electric service had to be suspended, and in 1900 the dam burst, flooding the city.

Young men at the University of Texas began playing football in 1893, whenever they could find an opposing team willing to meet for a game. The team played its first official intercollegiate game in October 1894 against Texas A&M University. The Austin team won 38 to 0, beginning a football rivalry that would continue for more than a century.

Streetcar Number 15, with its conductor and motormen, covered Rio Grande Street. The fare was 5 cents in 1891 and did not increase until 1920. Employee rules included: "Every employee must at all times give civil answers to all proper enquiries on the part of the public." Conductors and motormen used a system of bells to communicate. One clang from the conductor meant "Stop at next crossing." Two meant "Go ahead."

This photograph taken in 1897 shows Fulton's Ice Cream Parlor, at 1608 Lavaca Street. Austinites were treated to their first taste of ice cream in the summer of 1869, at Charles W. Ohrndorf's Ice Cream Saloon. The cold dessert became available only after ice could be made. For many years, ice cream was a treat reserved for special occasions, so perhaps the little girl pictured is celebrating her birthday.

Before the Austin Street Railway brought electric streetcars to Austin, "mass" transportation took the form of mule-drawn streetcars similar to this horse-drawn conveyance, which was called an "excursion car" in 1899.

This elite group, known as the Governor's Guard or the Harper Kerby Rifles, is undergoing inspection, probably at Camp Mabry in the late 1890s. Originally 90 acres, Camp Mabry grew in size during the turn of the century. The federal government purchased additional acreage for training the National Guard, some land was donated, and by 1911 the camp had grown to encompass 400 acres.

Texas Volunteer Guard troops (later the Texas National Guard) drill at Camp Mabry around 1898, preparing for action in the Spanish-American War. Camp Mabry had been founded in northwest Austin in 1892.

This busy barbershop in East Austin, owned and operated by and for African-Americans, was photographed around 1895. It displays the latest conveniences, such as individual wall-mounted lamps and motorized ceiling fans, for the benefit of its customers.

This view of Congress Avenue circa 1895 shows the Union Depot at the corner of Cypress (Third) Street with its recognizable rotunda (left), and the tracks for the electric streetcars, which began in 1891 running up and down the center of "the Avenue," powered by overhead cables connected to telegraph poles.

Proprietor Buck Miller takes a breath of fresh air outside the Silver King. Saloons of varying degrees of respectability were prevalent in Austin during the late 1800s, lending the town a somewhat unwholesome reputation among some Texans. It became the custom of proper ladies to avoid several blocks along Congress Avenue's east side because of the overflow of saloon patrons, some of whom also frequented the upstairs rooms for gambling.

Families and friends loved to pitch their tents and camp out at Zilker Park around the turn of the century. It was an era when leisure was a rather new concept, and most adults wore hats (or sunbonnets) outdoors, even when relaxing.

The Crescent, in the 1000 block of Congress Avenue, was one of several Austin ice cream parlors that flourished around the turn of the century. The Crescent was apparently so successful that the proprietors had their own company van, complete with advertising signage that featured their logo—a crescent moon and star.

# Era of Progress

## (1900–1919)

When the first dam collapsed in 1900, the waters of the Colorado River flooded the city for miles downstream, causing untold damage and loss of electrical power for months.

This photograph shows the aftermath of the 1900 flood on West Sixth Street.

This view of Sixth Street (formerly Pecan Street) after the turn of the century illustrates the transition period of transportation: automobiles and electric streetcars compete for space with pedestrians, bicycles, and horse-drawn wagons.

It was 1905 when Congress Avenue was paved for the first time—with brick. This event was viewed as Austin's debut as a bona fide city, rather than just a provincial town, and the bricking of Sixth Street quickly followed. Those who had automobiles, which began arriving in Austin around 1900, were thrilled, but buggy drivers and horse riders sometimes took spills when traveling too fast on the smooth new streets.

In May 1901, the 25th president of the United States, William McKinley, visited Austin, and thousands turned out to welcome him. A special arch was erected in his honor at the Capitol gate, and the president's carriage was accompanied by a military escort as he paraded up Congress Avenue. Four months later, Austin mourned when President McKinley was assassinated.

As the capital of Texas, Austin has often been honored by visits from nationally recognized politicians and dignitaries, including presidents. Always ready to make a speech, President Theodore "Teddy" Roosevelt is pictured speaking to Austinites from a specially decorated platform during his public appearance in 1905.

This view of Eleventh Street circa 1906 shows the Capitol grounds at left and the Travis County Courthouse, center, with the Methodist and Catholic church spires behind. To the right is a "moonlight tower" on Congress Avenue. By this time, the Lundberg Bakery had become Siglhofer's Bakery, as the sign on its side denotes, and its unique brass eagle is still visible.

Students of Sisters of the Holy Cross Parochial School (also called Guadalupe School) pose in costume for a performance celebrating U.S. independence. This school was operated by Our Lady of Guadalupe (Catholic) Church, which was founded in 1907 on East Ninth Street in East Austin, to minister to the growing Mexican-American community.

According to the signs, a fellow could get more than just a shave and a haircut at Reasonover's Central Barber Shop, pictured circa 1907.

A public gathering takes place on the grassy slopes of Wooldridge Park, which in 1909 became Austin's first of many parks. It covers one of four city blocks designated as public squares in Edwin Waller's original city plan and was named for Alexander Penn Wooldridge, Austin's progressive mayor and civic leader. With its central bandstand, the park was often the site of political rallies and outdoor concerts.

This is how Congress Avenue looked circa 1919. It appears that car parking was limited to the east side of the street at the time. The Majestic Theater (later renamed the Paramount) is on the right.

The fortresslike Travis County Jail stood in conveniently close proximity to the first Travis County Courthouse. Between the two was the jailer's house.

The chief of police, sheriff, and deputy sheriff pose on horseback, outfitted for a parade. By the beginning of the twentieth century, there were at least 20 members in the Austin police force. Under orders from Mayor Wooldridge, Chief of Police Will J. Morris (left) closed "Guy Town," the downtown red-light district, in 1913. It had flourished since the 1870s.

Austin law enforcement officers sit for a group photograph circa 1910, most of them dressed in distinctive uniforms. Fifth from left in the second row, with the white beard, is James P. Hart, commissioner of police.

The growing number of automobiles on Austin streets in the early 1900s warranted at least four policemen on motorbikes.

Posing in his richly appointed office in the Capitol, Governor Oscar Branch Colquitt displays all the trappings of a turn-of-the-century politician, including rolltop desk and spittoon. Colquitt was elected governor in 1910 as an anti-prohibitionist and reelected in 1912. His administration achieved advances in education, state institutions, and prison reform.

In the early 1900s, no self-respecting lady would allow herself to be seen in public without a "smart hat," and millinery shops such as this one did a thriving business in Austin.

The modest Speedway Saloon, owned by Otto Ulit (at left in apron, with his brother William), was named for the street on which it was located. Speedway—a northward extension of Congress Avenue through Hyde Park, the city's first residential suburb—was paid for by its developer, Monroe M. Shipe, who named it "the Speedway" because it led to the Hyde Park racetrack. "The" has long been dropped from the street's name.

In 1913, the Young Men's Business League (later to merge with the Austin Chamber of Commerce) posed in front of the building in which Civil War veteran "Doc" Mathews had his office. Two newspaper boys seem to be junior members. Roy Bedichek was league secretary then, before going on to become a beloved folklorist and writer, as well as a major organizer and promoter of the University Interscholastic League.

Newspapermen prepare to go to press in the *Statesman* office when it was on Congress Avenue between Seventh and Eighth streets. That space was replaced in 1915 by the Majestic Theater, later named the Paramount.

In October 1913, famed muckraker photographer Lewis Hine noted that this eight-year-old Austin newsboy, Albert Schafer, usually began selling Sunday papers at 8:00 A.M. Despite physical challenges, young Albert earned the grand sum of "one to two dollars a day." This photograph was part of Hine's documentation of working children undertaken for the National Child Labor Committee.

The city's first traffic cop, Officer Kelley, arrived from Atlanta in 1913 to direct Austin's increasing automobile traffic downtown. He stands at the intersection of Austin's two busiest paved thoroughfares, Sixth and Congress (note the trolley tracks). During rush hours, Kelley introduced Austin's first traffic light, which was battery powered and portable. Permanent electric traffic signals would not be installed until 1924.

Laguna Gloria, a Mediterranean-style villa overlooking Lake Austin on West Thirty-fifth Street, was built in 1916 on land that Stephen F. Austin had once planned as his homesite. It was the home of Henry H. Sevier and Clara Driscoll Sevier. In 1943, Clara conveyed the property to the Texas Fine Arts Association, and by 1966 it was Laguna Gloria Art Museum, specializing in educating Austinites of all ages about contemporary art.

Deep Eddy could boast the first open-air concrete swimming pool in Texas in 1916, when owner A. J. Eilers developed the natural-spring area as a tourist resort. The City of Austin purchased Deep Eddy from Eilers in 1935, when Austin's first WPA project began: construction of a $25,000 bath house for swimmers. The pool's cold spring water and tall shade trees still make it a popular spot on hot summer days.

After a destructive fire at the telephone office, telephone operators worked in temporary quarters. Austin was the site of the Southwest's first experimental telephone communication in 1877, when a minister's daughter sang "Almost Persuaded" from Dr. Clark's store in South Austin to the telegraph office on Congress Avenue, about six miles away. Austin claimed almost 5,000 telephones by 1916.

World War I doughboys pose circa 1916 in a graphic display of their nickname, the Cactus Division. General Woodford H. Mabry had introduced Austin spectators to military drills, dress parades, and battle enactments around 1891 at a military encampment near Hyde Park. The following year, Camp Mabry was founded as the Texas Volunteer Guard facility, often the site of displays for the public such as this one.

Penn Field, an aircraft-landing field south of Austin, was under construction circa 1917. Established for flight training by UT's School of Military Aeronautics, it was named for Austin cadet Eugene Doak Penn. Volunteers, including Boy Scouts and boys from the School for the Deaf, cleared the land of rocks and cornstalks. After World War I, the field was sold, and during the 1930s it housed the Woodward Furniture Factory.

This photograph taken at Penn Field after construction was complete shows a lineup of well-cared-for automobiles and early motorcycles. The men are World War I students at the School of Automobile Mechanics, circa 1918.

Signs such as this one at the American National Bank building were prevalent among Austin businesses during World War I, reminding citizens to do their part to help the war effort.

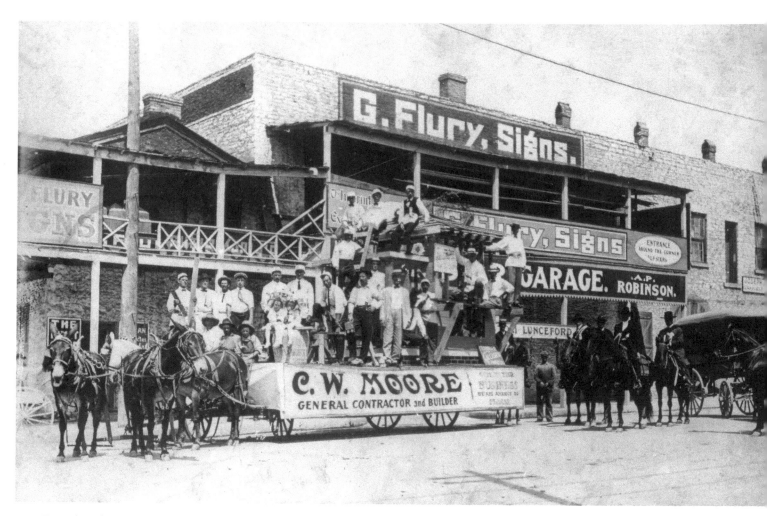

Even though automobiles were becoming more common, Austin's parades often featured teams of horses and mules. This parade float, sponsored by contractor and builder C. W. Moore circa 1918, featured carpenters on a miniature house they built expressly for the Labor Day parade.

When World War I ended with the armistice on November 11, 1918, Austinites quickly organized a Victory parade on Congress Avenue. Spectators gathered not only on both sides of the street but also in the middle along the streetcar tracks, and the parade moved both north and south. A privileged few watched from the Keystona Hotel's second-floor balcony, and almost everyone dressed up for the joyous occasion.

Standing on the steps of the first Travis County Courthouse, these well-dressed Austin women pose after registering to vote for the first time. The woman fourth from right, front row, is identified as Jane Y. McCallum, a president of the Austin Woman Suffrage Association who lobbied, spoke publicly, and wrote fervently to win full enfranchisement in 1919 for Texas women.

William Jennings Bryan—senator, three-time presidential candidate, and secretary of state—is believed to have lived in Austin between 1898 and 1899. This photograph shows his aides ("Senator Bryan's Boys") with local taxi drivers. Gifted at oratory, Bryan is best remembered in history for the 1925 Scopes "Monkey Trial" in Dayton, Tennessee, a staged contest between the ACLU and evolutionists against average, churchgoing Americans, represented by Bryan, waged to determine whether evolution or creation would be taught in public school classrooms.

Many people who come to Austin to attend the University of Texas, Huston-Tillotson College, Concordia College, or St. Edward's University decide that they want to stay in the city permanently. Consequently, Austin can boast a relatively well-educated population, and bookstores are popular haunts. Some thrive, but others come and go. This is the interior of Tobin's Book Store, one that went.

In the Paramount's heyday as a movie theater, it took several skilled hands to project the films without a hitch. Some of them are pictured here with their managers in what may be the basement of the theater.

# ELATION AND DEPRESSION

## (1920–1940)

This exterior view of the Paramount Theater circa 1920 shows its handsome architectural detailing in days when automobiles were still relatively new to Austin. The marquee seems remarkably subtle by today's standards. Built in 1915 by local banker Ernest Nalle, this "Picture Palace" was restored to its original glory and reopened during the downtown renaissance of the 1980s.

In 1921, surviving members of Terry's Texas Rangers, a company of Confederate cavalrymen during the Civil War, gathered at the foot of the statue erected in their honor on the Capitol grounds. Pictured in this reunion photograph are veterans from Austin and nearby towns, along with some of their female relatives.

Residents pose in 1921 in front of the Texas Confederate Home, opened in 1886 on West Sixth Street. Funds to establish this home for disabled and indigent veterans were raised by the John B. Hood Camp of United Confederate Veterans and the United Daughters of the Confederacy. Between 1887 and 1953, more than 2,000 former Confederates lived at the facility. The last resident, Thomas Riddle, died at age 108.

Photographed in the spring of 1921, field hands employed by the Crockett Produce Company's packing house prepare to board a train to the spinach field.

It looks as if these 1920s Austinites were so delighted by the visit of humorist Will Rogers that they couldn't drive straight! Rogers is wearing a hat and riding in the backseat of the convertible in the foreground, with his elbow on the ledge.

Employees of the Austin Street Railway Company gather in 1922 for a banquet at the elegant Driskill Hotel.

In 1923, students at Baker School won the Music Memory Contest (still being held annually) for three years in a row, which entitled them to keep the trophy. Baker School was built in Hyde Park in 1911.

Members of the Austin Fire Department pose with their vehicles in 1923. The hatted man not wearing a uniform, at center, is Fire Commissioner H. W. Nolan. In 1916, Austin voters had approved the change from a volunteer force to a paid force. The new fire department began with 27 fire fighters, 5 motorized vehicles, and 3 pieces of horse-drawn fire equipment left over from volunteer days.

University of Texas students circa the early 1920s study at Battle Hall, the university's original library. Designed in 1910 in the Spanish Renaissance style by architect Cass Gilbert, it was lauded as one of the finest buildings in the state. Battle Hall influenced the campus building style well into the 1930s. It was named for William James Battle, professor of Greek and acting president of UT from 1914 to 1916.

In April 1924, Prohibition in Austin was in full swing. This photograph shows Austin policemen and Texas Rangers after they seized 157 quarts of whiskey and other liquor. Pictured (from left) are officers R. R. Fowler, W. M. Bowden, O. B. Chesshir, L. D. McClain, A. H. Von Rosenberg, and W. E. Mayberry.

The Stephen F. Austin Hotel, distinguished by a balcony wrapping around two sides of the second-floor ballroom, opened in 1924 on Congress Avenue's east side. It later became the Bradford Hotel.

The proceeds from a productive oil well on West Texas land owned by the University of Texas initiated a building boom that dramatically expanded the Austin campus. On November 27, 1924, UT dedicated its Memorial Stadium during the annual Thanksgiving Day football game against Texas A&M University. The Texas A&M Aggies have traditionally been the main rivals of the University of Texas Longhorns.

Crowds gathered at Congress and Eleventh Street circa 1925 after a new streetcar derailed and overturned during its inaugural inspection tour by company directors. It was a rainy day. The older streetcar, behind the new streamlined model, is still upright. The Austin Street Railway Company, which introduced the city to mass transit with mule-drawn streetcars, served Austin for 50 years with its electric streetcars.

Among the nation's presidents who graced Austin with their presence was Calvin Coolidge ("Silent Cal"), pictured during his term of office (1923–1929) at a banquet in his honor. The president stands in front of the flag beside Mrs. Coolidge, who wears a chic hat.

It would appear that this South Austin drugstore circa 1925 offered almost everything a customer could possibly want—except, perhaps, a friendly smile.

Before there was a Goodyear blimp, there was the oversized Goodyear tire, purportedly the "World's Largest Tire," attached to the back of an early truck. This photograph shows the eye-catching advertising gimmick on a street in front of the Capitol.

Wearing their decorated picture hats, these members of the Ladies' Auxiliary to the Carpenters face the camera as their chauffeured car, covered with crepe-paper calla lilies, makes its way in a 1920s spring parade. Austin's penchant for parades, begun in the nineteenth century, has continued into the twenty-first.

The splendid 14-story Norwood Building, at 808 West Tenth Street, with its early Art Deco influence, was completed in 1929. It was Austin's first air-conditioned office building and boasted the city's first self-parking ramped automobile garage (called the Motoramp). Earlier parking garages had used large elevators to move cars up and down.

This view shows Congress Avenue, looking south from the corner of Seventh Street, probably in the late 1920s.

Members of the Travis County 4H Club and their sponsors parade on Congress Avenue in support of farms. Many of the members shown carry sapling trees for planting.

In October 1930, Austin's new Municipal Airport opened near the northeast section of town. It was dedicated in honor of former city councilman Robert Mueller and marked the beginning of airmail service for the city. This photograph shows the decidedly homey Braniff Airways terminal in 1938.

Members of the Austin Fire Department in 1930 display their shiny new firetruck at Fire Station Number Nine, located in Hyde Park.

During the Depression years, first lady Eleanor Roosevelt served as goodwill ambassador for the administration of her husband, Franklin D. Roosevelt. She (the tallest) was photographed while meeting with some of Austin's leading women (from left): Mrs. W. R. Long, Velma Hunter, Mint Reed, Nina Bremond, Camille Butler, Dot Wilcox, Lutie Perry, and Mrs. Bickler.

Hirsh's Drug Store, pictured here in the Depression days, was on a busy corner of Congress Avenue.

This view shows how Congress Avenue appeared looking north on a rainy day in 1939, decorated for the inauguration of Governor W. Lee "Pappy" O'Daniel, self-proclaimed "hillbilly" singer and radio personality.

In December 1932, well-dressed young men and women pose near the dance floor during a holiday party at the Austin Country Club, located in the Tarrytown neighborhood west of downtown.

The appearance of Congress Avenue and other Austin commercial streets changed noticeably in the 1930s, when architecture began reflecting Art Moderne and Art Deco designs. Some structures, such as the new Austin National Bank, were built in the contemporary style, while others simply added modernized facades to existing nineteenth-century storefronts.

Harry Aiken, a former Hollywood actor, opened his first Night Hawk restaurant in 1933, emulating late-night cafes in California. He soon had several of them around town. This photograph shows employees at the second Night Hawk, on Guadalupe, popular with university students. In 1958, Aiken was the first Austin restaurateur to integrate, serving African-Americans years before any other local restaurant followed suit.

By 1934, when this photograph was taken, gasoline stations such as this Texaco in South Austin were common sights. Its next-door neighbor, the Frisco, was possibly the first of several such popular and locally owned hamburger cafes around town.

Dance students dressed as sylphs rehearse for a recital on the lawn at Eastwoods Park circa 1935. Many of the city's parks were enhanced by stonework structures and walls, created by stonemasons employed by the government through tax dollars during the Depression years. This park is located just north of the University of Texas campus.

Pictured circa 1934 is petite performer Sally Rand, posing on the Capitol steps in Hollywood's idea of a cowgirl outfit and surrounded by her welcoming committee. Miss Rand was a silent-screen actress in the 1920s, but she was best known for creating a sensation at the 1933 world's fair in Chicago by dancing with two large ostrich-plume fans—and what appeared to be nothing else. The man at far-left is identified as Wiley Post, famous aviator from Texas.

The Varsity Theater was across from the University of Texas campus, on the section of Guadalupe Street that has long been called "the Drag." This photo shows how the Varsity looked in 1936, when Dick Powell and Joan Blondell were Hollywood stars and Borden's ice cream and soda-fountain shop was next door.

DID YOU KNOW THAT THE WATER,
LIGHT, & SEWER DEPARTMENT EMPLOYES 275 MEN & WOMEN.
THAT ELECTRICITY NOW COST YOU 40% LESS THAN 10 YEARS AGO.
THAT ONE FIFTH OF ALL ELECTRICITY PRODUCED IS USED IN PUMPING
WATER, LIGHT IN YOUR SCHOOLS, STREETS, PLAYGROUNDS, ETC.
CITY OF AUSTIN

This City of Austin parade truck in the 1930s featured a sign reminding citizens just how fortunate they were to have an efficient system of water, electricity, and sewage disposal—even when days of the Great Depression were tough.

As if the Great Depression were not stressful enough, the Colorado River flooded in 1935.

In 1936, President Franklin
D. Roosevelt made a brief
whistle-stop in Austin
while on a railway tour.
Despite the late hour of the
train's arrival, thousands
of Austinites turned out
to greet the president and
first lady, Eleanor. Before
leaving, FDR touched off
a ceremonial dynamite
explosion to break ground
for the Texas Memorial
Museum.

This bird's-eye view of the University of Texas campus shows the 307-foot tower of the Administration building, completed in 1937. The homogeneous architectural style of the campus buildings constructed in the 1930s were inspired by Cass Gilbert's Spanish Renaissance design of Battle Hall. The university's building boom and other construction projects helped keep many Austinites employed during the Depression years.

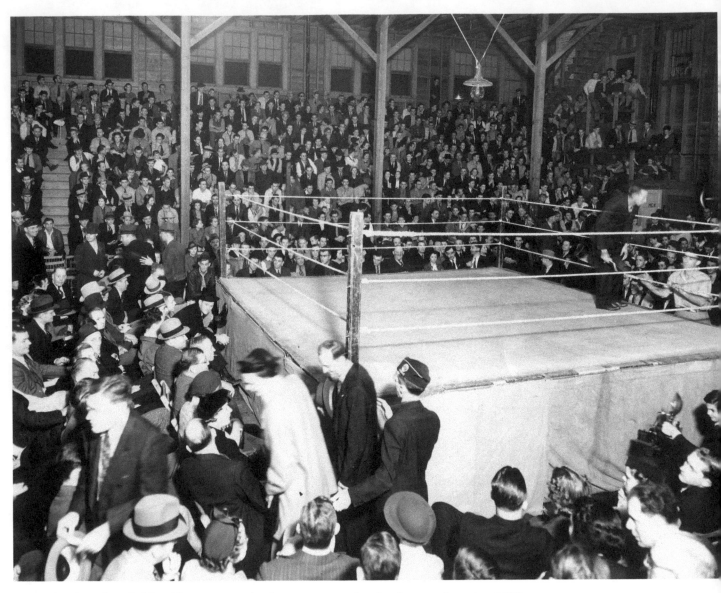

A crowd gathers for a Golden Gloves amateur boxing tournament in a local gymnasium circa 1938.

At one-forty in the afternoon of February 7, 1940, Austinites gathered at Congress Avenue and Sixth Street for a last ride on the city's electric streetcars. This day meant a significant change in the lives of Austin commuters, who from then on would be riding the Austin Transit Company's new buses, rather than the streetcars that had served the city in one form or another since 1875.

Looking down Sixth Street from the center of Congress circa 1940, one couldn't miss the Littlefield Building's curved facade (left) and the Driskill Hotel right behind it. In this view, the trolley tracks have been removed and paved over.

This photograph shows the interior of the City Book Store, where apparently cigars as well as books were sold and film developing was another sideline. The sign at left, "Join Our Circulating Library," indicates that the picture may have been taken before 1926, when the American Association of University Women started Austin's first library.

The Governor's Mansion, 1010 Colorado Street, is conveniently located within a block of the Capitol. Designed by local renowned architect Abner Cook in the Greek Revival style, it was completed in 1856. Its first resident was Governor Elisha Marshall Pease, and it has been the official home of the governors of Texas ever since. A rear addition was completed in 1914 during Governor Colquitt's term.

Judge Sebron G. Sneed acquired 470 acres south of Austin in 1854 and built this imposing 12-room house in 1857 with the aid of a mason and a carpenter. The limestone was quarried on the property by slaves, and the house featured eight fireplaces. Sneed brought his family and possessions from Arkansas to Austin by oxcart, and he was one of Austin's most respected criminal lawyers before becoming a judge.

Swedish immigrant Charles Lundberg completed his New Orleans Bakery in 1876, soon adding an ice cream parlor and a huge bread oven. His chosen location on Congress Avenue was ideal, a mere stone's throw from the Capitol. Although the building changed hands several times after Lundberg's death, it remained a bakery until 1937. It is still known locally as the Lundberg Bakery building.

# War, Peace, and Activism

## (1941–1969)

By 1945, Congress Avenue's old brick paving had long since been covered over with modern paving to withstand the traffic of automobiles, buses, and motorcycles. The corner in front of Woolworth's was a popular bus stop for downtown workers. The locally owned Scarbrough's Department Store was in the tall building at center, the city's first "skyscraper" of eight stories.

Members of the Women's Army Corps (and others) pose for a photographer at Camp Mabry during World War II. Military personnel also were stationed at Bergstrom Air Force Base, formerly Del Valle Army Air Field, and at Camp Swift, outside Bastrop, Texas, a nearby town east of Austin.

In the postwar years through the 1960s, drive-in movie theaters, located on spacious lots away from the center of town, were the precursors of watching movies at home on television and almost as comfortable. Austin's Chief Drive-In Theater featured, appropriately, a Texas longhorn steer as its design motif on the back of its mammoth screen in 1952.

In the postwar years of the late 1940s and early 1950s, retail businesses on Congress Avenue—including clothing stores, Sears, and Renfro's Rexall Drug Store—were prospering. But suburbs were proliferating as well, and soon they would draw business away from the original downtown area.

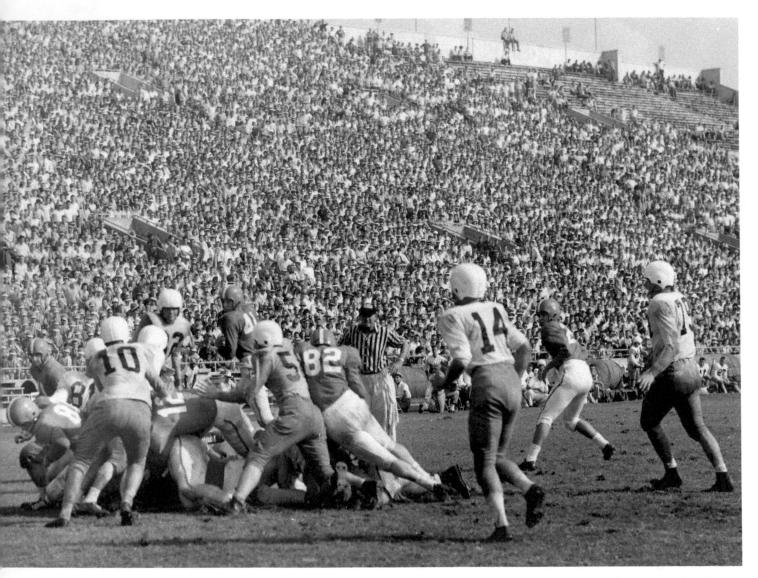

As the crowded stands clearly indicate, football was a favorite spectator sport at the University of Texas in the 1950s and 1960s. In December 1969, President Richard M. Nixon proclaimed the undefeated UT Longhorns the Number One college football team in the country.

Presidential candidate John F. Kennedy receives a sombrero during a 1960 campaign stop in Austin with running mate Lyndon B. Johnson.

Visiting Austin in 1964, Hollywood leading man Gregory Peck (right), winner of the Academy Award for his performance in 1962's *To Kill a Mockingbird,* receives a signed Longhorn football from famed University of Texas coach Darrell K. Royal (center). Peck was presented with the key to the city as well. The university's Memorial Stadium would later be renamed in honor of Coach Royal.

With his own hands, no blueprints, and minimal assistance, Austinite Isamu Taniguchi created the peaceful Oriental Gardens and Teahouse at Zilker Park as his gift to the city. He completed the three-acre project in 1969. Taniguchi persuaded local businesses to donate everything needed for the site. It features waterfalls, paths, handhewn bridges, and six ponds subtly shaped to spell AUSTIN when viewed from above.

The Eugene Bremond House, 404 West Seventh Street, was the first home built in what is now the Bremond Block Historic District, developed by the Bremond and Robinson families from the 1860s through the 1890s. Designed by local contractor George Fiegel, the Victorian house with a raised basement features surrounding porches ornamented with pairs of slender square columns. Eugene Bremond was a prominent Austin banker.

Congress Avenue is always decorated for the holidays. This nighttime photograph looking south toward the river shows the avenue covered in a blaze of lights in the 1960s.

# Notes on the Photographs

These notes, listed by page number, attempt to include all aspects known of the photographs. Each of the photographs is identified by the page number, a title or description, photographer and collection, archive, and call or box number when applicable. Although every attempt was made to collect all data, in some cases complete data may have been unavailable due to the age and condition of some of the photographs and records.

II   **POST OFFICE**
1932/5-191   TEXAS STATE LIBRARY & ARCHIVES COMMISSION

VI   **THE BEN HUR**
PICA 13016
AUSTIN HISTORY CENTER

X   **CONGRESS AVENUE**
PICA 02442
AUSTIN HISTORY CENTER

2   **HOOK AND LADDER COMPANY**
1932/5-163   TEXAS STATE LIBRARY & ARCHIVES COMMISSION

3   **STATE LUNATIC ASYLUM**
PICA 04382
AUSTIN HISTORY CENTER

4   **WESLEY CHAPEL METHODIST EPISCOPAL CHURCH**
1932/5-189   TEXAS STATE LIBRARY & ARCHIVES COMMISSION

5   **FRAME BUILDINGS ON PECAN STREET**
PICA 26344
AUSTIN HISTORY CENTER

6   **FIRST BALE OF COTTON SHIPPED BY RAIL**
PICA 04660
AUSTIN HISTORY CENTER

7   **TRAVIS COUNTY COURTHOUSE**
1932/5-195   TEXAS STATE LIBRARY & ARCHIVES COMMISSION

8   **PECAN STREET IN 1879**
PICA 01977
AUSTIN HISTORY CENTER

9   **PUBLIC HOSPITAL**
C 00053
AUSTIN HISTORY CENTER

10   **WORKERS WITH STATUE OF GODDESS**
1989/90-1 TEXAS STATE LIBRARY & ARCHIVES COMMISSION

11   **OLD MAIN**
CO 6713
AUSTIN HISTORY CENTER

12   **TEMPLE BETH ISRAEL**
C 01281
AUSTIN HISTORY CENTER

13   **MARKET CENTER OF PECAN STREET**
1932/5-117   TEXAS STATE LIBRARY & ARCHIVES COMMISSION

14   **CORPORATION BRIDGE**
1932/5-186   TEXAS STATE LIBRARY & ARCHIVES COMMISSION

15   **CAPITOL DEDICATION**
PICA 03075
AUSTIN HISTORY CENTER

16   **VIEW ON CONGRESS AVENUE**
PICA 18625
AUSTIN HISTORY CENTER

17   **TEXAS CAPITOL**
PICA 27295
AUSTIN HISTORY CENTER

18   **VIEW LOOKING SOUTH FROM CAPITOL DOME**
PICA 19498
AUSTIN HISTORY CENTER

19   **SOUTHWEST VIEW FROM CAPITOL DOME**
PICA 01092
AUSTIN HISTORY CENTER

20   **LOOKING EAST FROM CAPITOL DOME**
PICA 01096
AUSTIN HISTORY CENTER

21   **LOOKING WEST FROM CAPITOL DOME**
PICA 01100
AUSTIN HISTORY CENTER

22   **CONGRESS AVENUE IN EARLY 1890s**
CO 0027
AUSTIN HISTORY CENTER

23   **ARCHWAY ACROSS CONGRESS AVENUE**
1932/5-80 TEXAS STATE LIBRARY & ARCHIVES COMMISSION

24   **GEM LAKE**
PICA 02642
AUSTIN HISTORY CENTER

25   **AUSTIN NATIONAL BANK**
PICA 02864
AUSTIN HISTORY CENTER

26 FIRST NATIONAL BANK
1932/5-190
TEXAS STATE LIBRARY &
ARCHIVES COMMISSION

27 MEN LAYING STREETCAR
TRACKS
PICA 02460
AUSTIN HISTORY CENTER

28 HYDE PARK TRANSIT
PAVILION
CO 1092
AUSTIN HISTORY CENTER

29 CONSTRUCTION OF
AUSTIN DAM
PICA 13076
AUSTIN HISTORY CENTER

30 UNIVERSITY OF TEXAS
FOOTBALL
PICA 19720
AUSTIN HISTORY CENTER

31 STREETCAR NUMBER 15
PICA 10571
AUSTIN HISTORY CENTER

32 FULTON'S ICE CREAM
PARLOR
CO 01086
AUSTIN HISTORY CENTER

33 EXCURSION CAR
CO 0732
AUSTIN HISTORY CENTER

34 GOVERNOR'S GUARD
PICA 06602
AUSTIN HISTORY CENTER

35 TEXAS VOLUNTEER
GUARD TROOPS
PICA 06993
AUSTIN HISTORY CENTER

36 BARBERSHOP IN EAST
AUSTIN
PICA 13518
AUSTIN HISTORY CENTER

37 UNION DEPOT
PICA 02530
AUSTIN HISTORY CENTER

38 SILVER KING SALOON
PICA 20951
AUSTIN HISTORY CENTER

39 ZILKER PARK
PICA 20150
AUSTIN HISTORY CENTER

40 THE CRESCENT
PICA 25953
AUSTIN HISTORY CENTER

42 DAM COLLAPSE
FLOODING
PICA 03994
AUSTIN HISTORY CENTER

43 1900 FLOOD
PICA 01979
AUSTIN HISTORY CENTER

44 TRANSPORTATION ON
SIXTH STREET
CO 0625
AUSTIN HISTORY CENTER

45 PAVING CONGRESS
AVENUE
C 00606
AUSTIN HISTORY CENTER

46 PRESIDENT MCKINLEY'S
VISIT
1932/5-4, 5, 6, AND 7
TEXAS STATE LIBRARY &
ARCHIVES COMMISSION

47 PRESIDENT THEODORE
ROOSEVELT SPEAKING TO
AUSTINITES
PICA 17440
AUSTIN HISTORY CENTER

48 ELEVENTH STREET
PICA 04776
AUSTIN HISTORY CENTER

49 GUADALUPE SCHOOL
PICA 25921
AUSTIN HISTORY CENTER

50 REASONOVER'S CENTRAL
BARBER SHOP
PICA 18518
AUSTIN HISTORY CENTER

51 WOOLDRIDGE PARK
C 06049
AUSTIN HISTORY CENTER

52 MAJESTIC THEATER
CO 2068
AUSTIN HISTORY CENTER

53 TRAVIS COUNTY JAIL
CO 2377
AUSTIN HISTORY CENTER

54 LAWMEN ON HORSEBACK
PICA 18342
AUSTIN HISTORY CENTER

55 POLICE GROUP PHOTO
PICA 01425
AUSTIN HISTORY CENTER

56 POLICEMEN ON
MOTORBIKE
PICA 01403
AUSTIN HISTORY CENTER

57 GOVERNOR OSCAR
BRANCH COLQUITT
CO 0311
AUSTIN HISTORY CENTER

58 MILLINERY SHOP
PICA 15505
AUSTIN HISTORY CENTER

59 SPEEDWAY SALOON
PICB 12557
AUSTIN HISTORY CENTER

60 YOUNG MEN'S BUSINESS
LEAGUE
CO 0014
AUSTIN HISTORY CENTER

61 PRESSMEN AT
STATESMAN OFFICE
1932/5 -17
TEXAS STATE LIBRARY &
ARCHIVES COMMISSION

62 NEWSIE
LIBRARY OF CONGRESS
PHOTO

63 OFFICER KELLEY
C 00650
AUSTIN HISTORY CENTER

64   LAGUNA GLORIA
     C 01564
     AUSTIN HISTORY CENTER

65   DEEP EDDY
     C 01786
     AUSTIN HISTORY CENTER

66   TELEPHONE OPERATORS
     CO 3142
     AUSTIN HISTORY CENTER

67   WORLD WAR I
     DOUGHBOYS
     PICA 03334
     AUSTIN HISTORY CENTER

68   PENN FIELD UNDER
     CONSTRUCTION
     PICA 18500
     AUSTIN HISTORY CENTER

69   PENN FIELD
     PICA 19213
     AUSTIN HISTORY CENTER

70   WAR SIGNS
     C 11060
     AUSTIN HISTORY CENTER

71   LABOR DAY FLOAT
     PICA 10984
     AUSTIN HISTORY CENTER

72   VICTORY PARADE
     CO 0261
     AUSTIN HISTORY CENTER

73   AUSTIN WOMEN
     REGISTER TO VOTE
     PICA 11669
     AUSTIN HISTORY CENTER

74   BRYAN'S BOYS
     PICA 07048
     AUSTIN HISTORY CENTER

75   TOBIN'S BOOK STORE
     CO 5670
     AUSTIN HISTORY CENTER

76   PROJECTIONISTS AT
     PARAMOUNT THEATER
     CO 6825
     AUSTIN HISTORY CENTER

78   EXTERIOR OF
     PARAMOUNT THEATER
     CO 1138
     AUSTIN HISTORY CENTER

79   TERRY'S TEXAS RANGERS
     CO 4897
     AUSTIN HISTORY CENTER

80   TEXAS CONFEDERATE
     HOME
     CO 3676
     AUSTIN HISTORY CENTER

81   CROCKETT PRODUCE
     COMPANY
     CO 6333
     AUSTIN HISTORY CENTER

82   WILL ROGERS
     CO 9944
     AUSTIN HISTORY CENTER

83   STREET RAILWAY
     COMPANY DINNER
     PICA 24857
     AUSTIN HISTORY CENTER

84   BAKER SCHOOL
     STUDENTS
     PICA 25404
     AUSTIN HISTORY CENTER

85   AUSTIN FIRE
     DEPARTMENT
     PICA 02859
     AUSTIN HISTORY CENTER

86   BATTLE HALL
     PICA 20492
     AUSTIN HISTORY CENTER

87   PROHIBITION SEIZURE
     PICA 29216
     AUSTIN HISTORY CENTER

88   STEPHEN F. AUSTIN
     HOTEL
     CO 8993
     AUSTIN HISTORY CENTER

89   MEMORIAL STADIUM
     CO9993B
     AUSTIN HISTORY CENTER

90   STREETCAR DERAILMENT
     CO 0598
     AUSTIN HISTORY CENTER

91   PRESIDENT CALVIN
     COOLIDGE
     PICA 07057
     AUSTIN HISTORY CENTER

92   SOUTH AUSTIN
     DRUGSTORE
     PICA 15160
     AUSTIN HISTORY CENTER

93   WORLD'S LARGEST TIRE
     CO 6616
     AUSTIN HISTORY CENTER

94   LADIES' AUXILIARY TO
     THE CARPENTERS
     CO8678
     AUSTIN HISTORY CENTER

95   NORWOOD BUILDING
     PICA 00344
     AUSTIN HISTORY CENTER

96   CONGRESS AVENUE IN
     THE LATE 1920s
     CO 0645
     AUSTIN HISTORY CENTER

97   TRAVIS COUNTY 4H CLUB
     PARADE
     CO 8690
     AUSTIN HISTORY CENTER

98   MUNICIPAL AIRPORT
     PICA 03771
     AUSTIN HISTORY CENTER

99   FIRE STATION NUMBER
     NINE
     CO 3254
     AUSTIN HISTORY CENTER

100  ELEANOR ROOSEVELT
     PICA 07070
     AUSTIN HISTORY CENTER

101  HIRSH'S DRUG STORE
     CO 0666
     AUSTIN HISTORY CENTER

102 INAUGURATION PARADE
CO 0620
AUSTIN HISTORY CENTER

103 PARTY AT AUSTIN
COUNTRY CLUB
CO 7796
AUSTIN HISTORY CENTER

104 AUSTIN NATIONAL BANK
PICA 02726
AUSTIN HISTORY CENTER

105 NIGHT HAWK
RESTAURANT
PICA 28695
AUSTIN HISTORY CENTER

106 TEXACO STATION
C11292
AUSTIN HISTORY CENTER

107 EASTWOODS PARK
CO 1779
AUSTIN HISTORY CENTER

108 SALLY RAND
CO 2862
AUSTIN HISTORY CENTER

109 VARSITY THEATER
PICA 06734
AUSTIN HISTORY CENTER

110 PARADE TRUCK
PICA 33279
AUSTIN HISTORY CENTER

111 FLOOD OF 1935
CO 8484-A
AUSTIN HISTORY CENTER

112 PRESIDENT FRANKLIN D.
ROOSEVELT
PICA 25665
AUSTIN HISTORY CENTER

113 UNIVERSITY OF TEXAS
ADMINISTRATION
BUILDING
PICA 07782
AUSTIN HISTORY CENTER

114 GOLDEN GLOVES MATCH
PICA 23531
AUSTIN HISTORY CENTER

115 LAST STREETCAR RIDE
CO 0056
AUSTIN HISTORY CENTER

116 LITTLEFIELD BUILDING
PICA 01993
AUSTIN HISTORY CENTER

117 CITY BOOK STORE
1932/5-19 TEXAS STATE
LIBRARY & ARCHIVES
COMMISSION

118 GOVERNOR'S MANSION
HABS No. TEX-3304
LIBRARY OF CONGRESS

119 SNEED HOUSE
HABS No. TEX-399
LIBRARY OF CONGRESS

120 LUNDBERG BAKERY
HABS No.TEX-3267-1
LIBRARY OF CONGRESS

122 SCARBROUGH'S
DEPARTMENT STORE
CO 3182
AUSTIN HISTORY CENTER

123 WAC MEMBERS AT CAMP
MABRY
PICA 28622
AUSTIN HISTORY CENTER

124 CHIEF DRIVE-IN THEATRE
PICA 27706
AUSTIN HISTORY CENTER

125 CONGRESS AVENUE IN
POSTWAR YEARS
CO 0581
AUSTIN HISTORY CENTER

126 UNIVERSITY OF TEXAS
FOOTBALL
C10110
AUSTIN HISTORY CENTER

127 PRESIDENT JOHN F.
KENNEDY
AS 60-2876
AUSTIN HISTORY CENTER

128 GREGORY PECK
PICA 16276
AUSTIN HISTORY CENTER

129 ORIENTAL GARDENS
AAS 74038B
AUSTIN HISTORY CENTER

130 EUGENE BREMOND
HOUSE
HABS No. TEX-3143
LIBRARY OF CONGRESS

131 CONGRESS AVENUE AT
CHRISTMAS
PICA 10595
AUSTIN HISTORY CENTER

Printed in the USA
CPSIA information can be obtained
at www.ICGtesting.com
JSHW072023140824
68134JS00042B/3756